GLORIA COPELAND

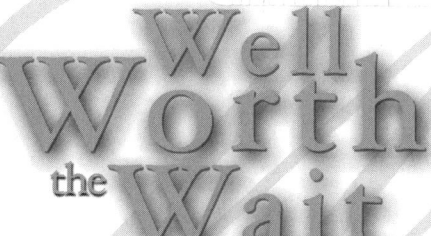

Well Worth the Wait

KENNETH
COPELAND
PUBLICATIONS

Unless otherwise noted, all scripture is from the *King James Version* of the Bible.

Scripture quotations marked *The Amplified Bible* are from *The Amplified Bible, Old Testament* © 1965, 1987 by The Zondervan Corporation. *The Amplified New Testament* © 1958, 1987 by The Lockman Foundation. Used by permission.

Well Worth the Wait

ISBN 0-88114-980-2   30-0535

08 07 06 05 04 03   12 11 10 09 08 07

© 1995 Kenneth Copeland Ministries, Incorporated

Kenneth Copeland Publications
Fort Worth, Texas 76192-0001

For more information about Kenneth Copeland Ministries, call 1-800-600-7395 or visit www.kcm.org.

Well Worth the Wait

The pressure is on.

You have prayed the prayer of faith. You believe you have received the answer. You are confessing the Word. You are standing on God's promise. You are expecting a miracle.

But instead of getting better— things seem to get worse. Symptoms and circumstances pile up around you. Every time you turn around, some demon is whining in your ear: *Why don't you just give up? This faith stuff doesn't work. God doesn't even care about you.*

Soon all you can think about is how tired you are, and how fed up you are with waiting for your answer to come. You have had it with this situation and unless something changes, you're about to say the two words that cost more believers their victory than anything else in the world: *I quit!*

Sound familiar?

Sure it does. Everyone who ever walked by faith has gone through times like that. Tough times. Times when you feel like you can't take any more.

Maybe those times have tripped you up in the past. Maybe the devil has used them to pressure you into letting go of your faith. But I want you to know something today. That never has to happen again because you're about to learn how to release a force so powerful it can carry you through those hard times in triumph.

It is a force so dynamic the devil

cannot stop it. It is a force that comes from the heart and character of God Himself and it will take you from here to victory...every time.

What is this magnificent force? The force of patience.

Standard Equipment

Most Christians have no idea how powerful patience actually is. They think it's just a nice quality. But, the fact is, patience is the overcoming force that keeps us going in situations that otherwise would stop us cold.

It's patience, for example, that will see you through from the time you pray and release your faith for your healing...to the time when that healing is a manifest reality in your body. It's patience that will take you from the moment you believe and confess by faith that your bills are paid...to the time when the money is finally in your account and you're writing the checks.

Contrary to popular belief, however, patience isn't simply putting up with a situation. It isn't hanging on by your fingernails until the bitter end. No, biblical patience is much greater than that.

Patience is the force that keeps you from fainting under pressure. It is the quality that does not surrender to circumstances or succumb under trial. Patience girds up your faith when it's under pressure. It refuses despondency even when conditions are dark, and holds to hope instead.

Patience suffers long and remains steadfast when distress and trouble come. It endures ill treatment without anger or thought of revenge. Patience keeps your faith from folding up when the going gets tough.

No matter what, patience just won't quit.

"That sounds great, Gloria," you may say. "But I don't have that kind of patience!"

If you've made Jesus the Lord of your life you do! It's a fruit of the Spirit and God equipped you with it the moment you were born again. He placed it into your recreated human spirit right along with the other fruit of the Spirit (see Galatians 5:22-23).

God didn't just give you any old type of patience, either. He imparted to you His very own patience, and *The Amplified Bible* says He is *extraordinarily* patient. God has what it takes to get through hard times. He has the power to persevere until circumstances line up with His Word. And because you're born of His

Spirit, you have that power too!

You may be thinking, *Where is all this wonderful patience I'm supposed to have? I certainly haven't seen much evidence of it in my life!*

It's waiting inside you for you to yield to it.

You see, just as water won't flow from a faucet unless you open the valve and let it through, the reservoir of patience God has put within you won't flow unless you release it by an act of your will.

As James 1:4 says you must *"let patience have her perfect work."* In other words, the force of patience won't go to work until you let it!

Count It All *What?*

It's only fair to warn you that's not always as easy as it may sound because patience is developed during tests and trials. You need it most when you want it least.

Let's look again at what James has to say about it:

> My brethren, count it all joy when ye fall into divers temptations; knowing this, that the trying of your faith worketh patience. But let patience have her perfect work, that ye may be perfect and entire, wanting nothing (James 1:2-4).

Usually, when you're in the midst of a trial, the last thing you feel like doing is counting it all joy. Naturally speaking, you're not in the mood to jump and sing and rejoice over this opportunity to develop patience.

But the truth is, you should.

Why? Because if you'll let patience

have her perfect work, you'll be perfect and entire, wanting nothing. Think about what that means! It means that if you're battling illness and you let patience have her perfect work, you'll end up in perfect health. If you're in financial trouble, you'll end up with all your needs perfectly met.

It means you'll end up with whatever the Word of God has promised you!

Hebrews 10 confirms that. Addressing a group of people who had been through an extremely fiery trial, it says:

Call to remembrance the former days, in which, after ye were illuminated, ye endured a great fight of afflictions; partly, whilst ye were made a gazingstock both by reproaches and afflictions; and partly, whilst ye became companions of them that were so used. For ye had compassion of me in my bonds, and took joyfully the spoiling of your goods, knowing in yourselves that ye have in heaven a better and an enduring substance. Cast not away therefore your confidence, which hath great recompence of reward. For ye have need of patience, that, after ye have done the will of God, ye might receive the promise (verses 32-36).

Read that last verse again: *"Ye have need of patience, that...ye might receive the promise."*

You might as well know right now that if you want to enjoy the health, deliverance and prosperity God has promised you, you'll have to let patience work. You'll have to believe God when it's hard to do. You'll have to keep walking in faith when your flesh just wants to quit.

That may sound negative, but it's not. It's just the truth. And if you know that truth, you can prepare yourself in advance for those hard times by deciding that when they come, you won't give up. You can train yourself for victory by starting right now to develop the force of patience you'll need to make it through when the going gets tough.

Growing in the Grocery Store

You see, you don't have to wait for a major trial to hit before you let patience have her perfect work. You can practice patience in those small but irritating situations you encounter every day.

I ran into one such situation just the other day in the grocery store. I was in a hurry when I went to check out so I chose the express line. There were only a couple of people in it and they just had a few items to buy so I didn't think it would take long.

But that clerk was so slow! As my frustration mounted I thought, *They ought to put a sign here that says Slow Motion Line!*

What was that? An opportunity to exercise patience.

Such opportunities are important because when you exercise patience, it grows. If you'll use it in small things, it will be strong enough to handle the bigger things when they come along. Every fruit of the Spirit increases in you as you exercise it.

Remember that the next time some little aggravation is about to make you lose your temper. Instead of saying, "I've had it," say, "No, in Jesus' Name, I choose to yield to the force of patience God has put within me. I believe I'll just count this slow grocery store line to be a joy and use it as an opportunity to grow!"

Risky Business

You may not think that sounds like much fun (and usually it's not) but I can tell you what is fun: *walking in victory!* It's fun to beat the devil and leave him crying in the dust while you walk away with the prize!

It's fun to win the race and, as Hebrews 12:1 says, patience helps us to do that:

> Wherefore seeing we also are compassed about with so great a cloud of witnesses, let us lay aside every weight, and the sin which doth so easily beset us, and let us run with patience the race that is set before us.

It's patience that will keep you running strong when you feel like lying down on the side of the road and letting the devil run over you. It's patience that will cause you to open your Bible when you are so discouraged you feel like having a television meltdown all day. It's patience that will keep you speaking words of faith instead of words of doubt and unbelief.

It's patience that will hold you steady in the basics of faith. And over the years, I've found it's those basics that will get you through even the most complicated situations. Victory comes when you simply persist in doing those things you know to do.

A few years ago, for example, this ministry fell behind financially—nearly $6 million of television bills behind! It looked to us like the answer to that problem was very complicated. We thought about selling all our ministry property and buildings so we could use the money to pay off the deficit. But then we wouldn't have any place to put our ministry operations.

Things looked dark. But do you know what got us through that situation? It wasn't some brilliant new revelation from God. It wasn't some flash from heaven bringing us an instant solution.

What overcame that deficit was the same thing that put food on our table more than 27 years ago when we first began to live by faith: a patient application of the Word of God.

I had our old reel-to-reel tapes of Kenneth E. Hagin's messages transferred to cassettes and listened to them again. We made a fresh application of the simple principles of confession he'd taught us so many years ago. We corrected ourselves concerning things we had let slip. We continued to make deposits of God's Word in our hearts and said the Word with our mouths.

In other words, we did what we knew to do. And just as James 1:4 says, that trial worked patience in us and when it was done, we lacked nothing. Not only was the deficit paid off—we haven't been behind financially since that time. Victory is so sweet!

What's more, the testimony of that particular victory has encouraged other ministers in similar situations.

That's the risk the devil always takes when he puts you through a trial. He takes the chance you'll come through in victory and end up stronger than you were before instead of weaker. He takes the chance of giving you another testimony of the miracle-working power of God.

Talk...Talk...Talk

That's why Satan works so hard to keep you from walking in patience. That's why he pressures you to quit. It's the only way he can defeat you!

So he talks...and talks...and talks. Like a salesman, he makes you a presentation and tries to sell you a bill of goods. He tells you God doesn't really love you. He tells you the Word isn't going to work this time. He tells you that you don't have the strength to go on. He'll even try to sell you on the idea that it would be easier for you just to curl up and die than to see this trial through in faith.

Now that talk can get very annoying but remember, that's *all* he can do! He doesn't have any real power or authority over you.

First Peter 5:8 says he walks

around as a roaring lion, *"seeking whom he may devour."* (Notice it doesn't say he is a lion. He just acts like one. And he can't devour you unless you let him.) *"Whom resist stedfast in the faith, knowing that the same afflictions are accomplished in your brethren that are in the world"* (verse 9).

How does that verse say you have to resist the devil? Steadfastly!

That means you have to use patience to resist him. He is, after all, a persistent fellow. He may pester you a thousand times a day, but if you'll resist him every time, he will flee from you every time (see James 4:7).

Does that surprise you?

It shouldn't. If you'll go to the Word of God and find out the actual truth about your situation, you'll find out the devil has no ability to withstand the divine power forces of faith and patience that God has put within you. He is just a defeated angel.

He and all the little low-level demons he sends to aggravate you have already *"come to nought"* (1 Corinthians 2:6). Jesus has stripped them of all their power and authority and left them with nothing.

You, however, are a new creature in Christ Jesus. You are born of God. You are filled with the Holy Spirit that proceeds from the Father. You're endowed with the Name of Jesus which is *"Far above all principality, and power, and might, and dominion, and every name that is named, not only in this world, but also in that which is to come"* (Ephesians 1:21).

"Greater is He that is in you, than he that is in the world!" (1 John 4:4)

That means your victory is guaranteed. The only way you can lose it is to quit. So don't do it.

Instead, yield to the powerful force of patience within you. Let it carry you through every trial—big and small. *"And after you have suffered a little while, the God of all grace...[Who imparts all blessing and favor], Who has called you to His [own] eternal glory in Christ Jesus, will Himself complete and make you what you ought to be, establish and ground you securely, and strengthen and settle you"* (1 Peter 5:10, *The Amplified Bible*).

In other words, He will make you perfect and entire, wanting nothing... and you'll gain a victory that is oh, so sweet!

Prayer for Salvation and Baptism in the Holy Spirit

Heavenly Father, I come to You in the Name of Jesus. Your Word says, "Whosoever shall call on the name of the Lord shall be saved" (Acts 2:21). I am calling on You. I pray and ask Jesus to come into my heart and be Lord over my life according to Romans 10:9-10. "If thou shalt confess with thy mouth the Lord Jesus, and shalt believe in thine heart that God hath raised him from the dead, thou shalt be saved. For with the heart man believeth unto righteousness; and with the mouth confession is made unto salvation." I do that now. I confess that Jesus is Lord, and I believe in my heart that God raised Him from the dead.

I am now reborn! I am a Christian— a child of Almighty God! I am saved! You also said in Your Word, "If ye then, being evil, know how to give good gifts unto your children: HOW MUCH MORE shall your heavenly Father give the Holy Spirit to them that ask him?" (Luke 11:13). I'm also asking You to fill me with the Holy Spirit. Holy Spirit, rise up within me as I praise God. I

fully expect to speak with other tongues as
You give me the utterance
(Acts 2:4). In Jesus' Name. Amen!

Begin to praise God for filling you with the Holy Spirit. Speak those words and syllables you receive—not in your own language, but the language given to you by the Holy Spirit. You have to use your own voice. God will not force you to speak. Don't be concerned with how it sounds. It is a heavenly language!

Continue with the blessing God has given you and pray in the spirit every day.

You are a born-again, Spirit-filled believer. You'll never be the same!

Find a good church that boldly preaches God's Word and obeys it. Become a part of a church family who will love and care for you as you love and care for them.

We need to be connected to each other. It increases our strength in God. It's God's plan for us.

Make it a habit to watch the *Believer's Voice of Victory* television broadcast and become a doer of the Word, who is blessed in his doing (James 1:22-25).

About the Author

Gloria Copeland is a noted author and minister of the gospel whose teaching ministry is known throughout the world. Believers worldwide know her through Believers' Conventions, Victory Campaigns, magazine articles, teaching tapes and videos, and the daily and Sunday *Believer's Voice of Victory* television broadcast, which she hosts with her husband, Kenneth Copeland. She is known for "Healing School," which she began teaching and hosting in 1979 at KCM meetings. Gloria delivers the Word of God and the keys to victorious Christian living to millions of people every year.

Gloria has written many books, including *God's Will for You, Walk With God, God's Will Is Prosperity, Hidden Treasures, Living Contact* and *Are You Listening?* She has also co-authored several books with her husband, including *Family Promises, Healing Promises* and the best-selling daily devotionals, *From Faith to Faith* and *Pursuit of His Presence.*

She holds an honorary doctorate from Oral Roberts University. In 1994, Gloria was voted Christian Woman of the Year, an honor conferred on women whose example demonstrates outstanding Christian leadership. Gloria is also the co-founder and vice president of Kenneth Copeland Ministries in Fort Worth, Texas.

Learn more about
Kenneth Copeland Ministries
by visiting our Web site at
www.kcm.org

Materials to Help You Receive Your Healing

by Gloria Copeland

Books

* And Jesus Healed Them All
  God's Prescription for Divine Health
* Harvest of Health
  Words That Heal (gift book with CD enclosed)

Audiotapes

God Is a Good God
God Wants You Well
Healing School

Videotapes

Healing School: God Wants You Well
Know Him as Healer

Books Available From
Kenneth Copeland Ministries

by Kenneth Copeland

* A Ceremony of Marriage
A Matter of Choice
Covenant of Blood
Faith and Patience—The Power Twins
* Freedom From Fear
Giving and Receiving
Honor—Walking in Honesty, Truth and Integrity
How to Conquer Strife
How to Discipline Your Flesh
How to Receive Communion
In Love There Is No Fear
Know Your Enemy
Living at the End of Time—A Time of Supernatural Increase
Love Never Fails
Managing God's Mutual Funds—Yours and His
Mercy—The Divine Rescue of the Human Race
* Now Are We in Christ Jesus
One Nation Under God (gift book with CD enclosed)
* Our Covenant With God
Partnership, Sharing the Vision—Sharing the Grace
* Prayer—Your Foundation for Success
* Prosperity: The Choice Is Yours
Rumors of War
* Sensitivity of Heart
* Six Steps to Excellence in Ministry
* Sorrow Not! Winning Over Grief and Sorrow
* The Decision Is Yours
* The Force of Faith
* The Force of Righteousness
The Image of God in You
The Laws of Prosperity

*Available in Spanish

The Power to Live a New Life
The Protection of Angels
The Unbeatable Spirit of Faith
*   Walk in the Spirit (Available in Spanish only)
Walk With God
Well Worth the Wait
Words That Heal (gift book with CD enclosed)
Your Promise of Protection—The Power of the 91st Psalm

Books Co-Authored by Kenneth and Gloria Copeland
Family Promises
Healing Promises
Prosperity Promises
Protection Promises

*   From Faith to Faith—A Daily Guide to Victory
From Faith to Faith—A Perpetual Calendar

One Word From God Series

- One Word From God Can Change Your Destiny
- One Word From God Can Change Your Family
- One Word From God Can Change Your Finances
- One Word From God Can Change Your Formula for Success
- One Word From God Can Change Your Health
- One Word From God Can Change Your Nation
- One Word From God Can Change Your Prayer Life
- One Word From God Can Change Your Relationships

Over The Edge—A Youth Devotional
Pursuit of His Presence—A Daily Devotional
Pursuit of His Presence—A Perpetual Calendar

Other Books Published by KCP
The First 30 Years—A Journey of Faith
    The story of the lives of Kenneth and Gloria Copeland.

*Available in Spanish

Real People. Real Needs. Real Victories.
  A book of testimonies to encourage your faith.
John G. Lake—His Life, His Sermons, His Boldness of Faith
The Holiest of All by Andrew Murray
The New Testament in Modern Speech by
  Richard Francis Weymouth
Unchained by Mac Gober

Products Designed for Today's Children and Youth

And Jesus Healed Them All! (confession book and CD gift package)
Baby Praise Board Book
Baby Praise Christmas Board Book
Noah's Ark Coloring Book
The Best of *Shout!* Adventure Comics
The *Shout!* Giant Flip Coloring Book
The *Shout!* Joke Book
The *Shout!* Super-Activity Book
Wichita Slim's Campfire Stories

*Commander Kellie and the Superkids*_{SM} Books:

The *SWORD* Adventure Book
*Commander Kellie and the Superkids*_{SM} Solve-It-
  Yourself Mysteries
*Commander Kellie and the Superkids*_{SM} Adventure Series
  Middle Grade Novels by Christopher P.N. Maselli
    #1 The Mysterious Presence
    #2 The Quest for the Second Half
    #3 Escape From Jungle Island
    #4 In Pursuit of the Enemy
    #5 Caged Rivalry
    #6 Mystery of the Missing Junk
    #7 Out of Breath
    #8 The Year Mashela Stole Christmas

*Available in Spanish

World Offices of
Kenneth Copeland Ministries

For more information about KCM and a free
catalog, please write the office nearest you:

Kenneth Copeland Ministries
Fort Worth, Texas 76192-0001

Kenneth Copeland
Locked Bag 2600
Mansfield Delivery Centre
QUEENSLAND 4122
AUSTRALIA

Kenneth Copeland
Post Office Box 15
BATH
BA1 3XN
U.K.

Kenneth Copeland
Private Bag X 909
FONTAINEBLEAU
2032
REPUBLIC OF
SOUTH AFRICA

Kenneth Copeland
Post Office Box 378
Surrey, B.C.
V3T 5B6
CANADA

Kenneth Copeland Ministries
Post Office Box 84
L'VIV 79000
UKRAINE

Believer's Voice of Victory
Television Broadcast

Join Kenneth and Gloria Copeland and the *Believer's Voice of Victory* broadcasts Monday through Friday and on Sunday each week, and learn how faith in God's Word can take your life from ordinary to extraordinary. This teaching from God's Word is designed to get you where you want to be—*on top!*

You can catch the *Believer's Voice of Victory* broadcast on your local, cable or satellite channels.

*Check your local listings for times and stations in your area.

Believer's Voice of Victory Magazine

Enjoy inspired teaching and encouragement from Kenneth and Gloria Copeland and guest ministers each month in the *Believer's Voice of Victory* magazine. Also included are real-life testimonies of God's miraculous power and divine intervention in the lives of people just like you!

It's more than just a magazine—it's a ministry.

Shout! The Voice of Victory for Kids

Shout!...The dynamic magazine just for kids is a Bible-charged, action-packed, quarterly magazine available FREE to kids everywhere! Featuring Wichita Slim and *Commander Kellie and the Superkids*_{SM}, *Shout!* is filled with colorful adventure comics, challenging games and puzzles, exciting short stories, solve-it-yourself mysteries and much more!!

Stand up, sign up and get ready to *Shout!*

To receive a FREE subscription to *Believer's Voice of Victory*, or to give a child you know a FREE subscription to *Shout!*, write to:

Kenneth Copeland Ministries
Fort Worth, Texas 76192-0001

Or call: 1-800-600-7395   (7 a.m.-5 p.m. CT)
Or visit our Web site at: **www.kcm.org**

If you are writing from outside the U.S., please contact the KCM office nearest you. Addresses for all Kenneth Copeland Ministries offices are listed on the previous pages.